The PLR Handbook: A No Fluff Guide On How To Profit With Private Label Rights

Disclaimer

This e-book has been written to provide information about self-improvement. Every effort has been made to make this ebook as complete and accurate as possible. However, there may be mistakes in typography or content. Also, this e-book provides information on self-improvement only up to the publishing date. Therefore, this ebook should be used as a guide - not as the ultimate source of web hosting information.

The purpose of this ebook is to educate. The author and the publisher does not warrant that the information contained in this e-book is fully complete and shall not be responsible for any errors or omissions. The author and publisher shall have neither liability nor responsibility to any person or entity with respect to any loss or damage caused or alleged to be caused directly or indirectly by this e-book.

Table of Contents

Introduction

The term "private label rights" (PLR) refers to a product that can be purchased and used or resold under the "brand" of the original purchaser. In everyday life, we encounter private label products very frequently—perhaps moreso than we might realize.

As an example, many supermarkets offer their own brand of soda or chips. Usually, the supermarket is not producing the soda or the chips using a proprietary approach and in a plant that they own. Rather, they are purchasing the chips and soda from a private label food products company, which creates them; and then delivers them to the supermarket either without any labels at all— or with the supermarket's own labels attached.

In the context of Internet marketing, the concept of private label rights (PLR) is a little more complicated, but it still captures the main idea inherent in the supermarket example. Generally, in IM, the term PLR is usually invoked in reference to intellectual property, such as ebooks, reports, articles, or some other form of written content, audio content, or video content.

And when it comes to intellectual property, things usually get a little more complicated. In the case of the supermarket selling private label soda, there aren't very many things to take into consideration. You buy the soda; you "re-brand it" by placing your own label on it; and you sell it to customers.

In the context of private label rights articles (a form of intellectual property), reselling the product in question might not be legally allowed by the contract you agree to when making the purchase. Instead, you might be restricted to using the articles for marketing purposes only. At the other extreme, the contract might grant you the right to resell the articles and resell the rights to resell the articles.

In general, picking articles that grant you desirable rights is an important part of making money with PLR. For this reason, I will defer this discuss to the next section, where I will talk about it in greater depth.

With all of this said, why should you care about PLR products? The simple answer is that they provide Internet marketers many promising opportunities. Creating a good product is generally a very large barrier to success for many

Internet marketers—one that often prevents new entrants to IM from ever experiencing success. But with the thick market for PLR products today, having your own product is as simple as purchasing one and rebranding it.

In the following sections, I will explain exactly how you can do this the right way. I will start by telling you what to look for when you purchase PLR products. After that, we will explore some of the many ways in which you can use those products to make money.

PLR Products Rights

In the introduction, we briefly and informally discussed the various types of "rights" that are granted to PLR package buyers. We will now consider these rights with a greater eye to detail.

Basic "Private Label Rights" (PLR)

In the most strict sense and in the context of IM, the term "PLR" usually refers to the most basic set of product rights available. As an example, consider the case where you purchase a package of 10 "PLR" articles. Usually, this means that you can legally…

1.   Modify the articles as desired
2.   Submit the articles to content directories, such as ezinearticles.com
3.   Place the articles on your own website
4.   Compile the articles into a report or ebook and sell that ebook or report

However, it is not always the case that a basic PLR package will include all four items. For instance, some PLR packages will not allow you to rebundle articles into ebooks or reports. For this reason, it is always a good idea to check out whether there are any special restrictions on the rights granted.

Resell Rights

After private label rights, the second most restrictive category is "resell rights." The difference between this and PLR should be obvious: you can take the article, ebook, or report that you purchase and resell it to others. In some cases, there will be restrictions on the quantity you can sell.

One important thing to note about resell rights is that there are either explicit or implicit restrictions on what your buyers can do with the articles. Usually, normal resell rights require that your buyers cannot resell the product once they purchase it from you. They may also be restricted in how they can use it (i.e. whether they can rebundle or alter it), too.

Master Resell Rights

The least restrictive set of rights you can get are "master resell rights." Usually, these will grant you all of the rights you would receive from basic PLR and resell rights licenses; however, they will also permit you to write your own license file.

This means that when you resell the product to your own buyers, you can allow them to do all or any of the following:

1.   Modify the articles as desired
2.   Submit the articles to content directories, such as ezinearticles.com
3.   Place the articles on their own website
4.   Compile the articles into a report or ebook and sell that ebook or report
5.   Resell the articles to new customers
6.   Allow those customers to resell the articles to additional customers
7.   Write their own license files

Of course, you don't need to offer all of these things to your customers; and, in fact, there are some instances in which it makes sense not to. We'll discuss these later.

Final Note on Types of Rights

Given the complexity of intellectual property, many PLR sellers have a custom license that carefully details what can and cannot be done legally with the product you can purchase. It is always a good idea to read over this carefully before making a purchase.

What Rights Should I Get?

After reading this section, it's natural to wonder what rights you should get. When doing this, there are two important things to keep in mind: 1) everyone else who purchases the package will also get the rights; and 2) you may need different rights for different projects.

The first consideration is more important than many PLR buyers realize. For instance, if your goal to purchase PLR articles, make slight modifications, and then upload them to your website for SEO purposes, then you'll want to buy PLR articles.

There are several reasons why you should do this, but one of them is the following: since everyone else only has basic private label rights, they will not be able to resell the articles or grant resell rights to them. This means the amount of people who will be using the same set of articles will be smaller; and the chances that you will be penalized for duplicate content will be lower.

To the contrary, if you own a PLR membership site; and your goal is to offer members content that they can use specifically for reports and ebooks, then duplicate content may not be as much of a problem. Additionally, you may want to give site visitors additional power to re-bundle, re-brand, and re-sell. For this reason, it might be a good idea to look for packages that offer resell rights or master resell rights.

Types of PLR Products

There are several different types of PLR products. The most commonly sold PLR product is a bundle of articles. These generally range in size from the very small packages you'll find on forums that are sold to a limited amount of individuals—to the very large packages you'll find for sale on various sites. These are usually sold to thousands of individuals and offer full master resell rights.

The benefit of selecting the large package is that you will be able to purchase hundreds or thousands of articles with re-branding, re-selling, and re-bundling rights for a very low price. The important disadvantage is that you will have to significantly modify the articles if you want to have any hope that they will appear to be unique content.

After PLR articles, ebooks and reports are probably the most common PLR products. Often, buyers purchase these products with the intent to either re-brand them and use them to sell affiliate products; or to use them to promote a website (i.e. by giving them away for free in exchange for joining a newsletter).

Finally, while Internet marketers do not usually buy and sell these types of PLR products frequently, audio, video, software, templates, and tangible products (such as DVD content, books, etc.) are also possible avenues for those interested in making money with PLR.

The Benefits of Using PLR

The benefits of using PLR products should be obvious. As an Internet marketer, you know how to market, but you don't necessarily know how to write a professional-quality report, ebook, or articles. This is truly the domain of writers or experts in your niche of choice; and, for this reason, it is a good idea to have someone else do the product-creation part for you.

Another benefit of using the PLR approach is that it is much cheaper than purchasing an entirely new product from a freelance writer. And if you do a good job selecting the source for your PLR content, few other people will be selling the same content, which means that it will be equally as effective.

A final benefit of using PLR content is that it will allow you to concentrate all of your time on marketing. Instead of taking the time to create an ebook outline, perform detailed research, and actually write and edit the ebook, you can simply start by purchasing; and from there, you can concentrate on getting it sold—or using it for whatever other purposes you had in mind.

Where to Find PLR Products

As we discussed previously, the source of your PLR content is critical. This will not only determine whether the products are well-written, well-researched, and well-composed, but it will also determine how many other people have access to it; and this can make all the difference.

While there are hundreds of sources of PLR content, many of them simply cannot offer you a package that is likely to earn you money. For this reason, I suggest that you use the following two sources, which I would personally recommend above all others:

1. http://plrwholesaler.com. This site offers PLR content in exchange for your email address, which is one of the best deals you'll find anywhere. To make things better, it has one of the greatest selections of PLR content available. Not only does it offer thousands of articles and dozens of ebooks, but it also offers IM-related software, Wordpress templates, and landing page prototypes.

2. http://unselfishmarketer.com. While you'll have to pay for access to this site, you'll get it at a great deal. You'll get dozens of high-quality software products, thousands of articles, and dozens of ebooks and reports. Additionally, the reach of the content will be limited, so that you won't need to worry as much about problems related to duplication.

Between these two sources, you should find enough PLR to start any project you have in mind.

How to Profit from PLR Products

There are dozens of different ways to profit from PLR products. In this section, I will cover the three broad categories of ways in which you can profit from PLR. In the following section, I will give a detailed overview of 20 specific methods.

Category #1: Use PLR Packages to Create Giveaway Products

As most Internet marketers know, giving stuff away for free can often be more profitable than trying to sell it. Free stuff can be used to get list subscribers and to circulate products with strong back-end sales devices. Free stuff can also be used to build rapport, so that future sales are easier to close.

Not surprisingly, many shrewd marketers are using PLR for this exact purpose: to create stuff that they can give away to site visitors and existing customers for free. This forms an important category of PLR product use. We will break this down further in the following section.

Category #2: Use PLR Products to Generate Traffic

This is another great use of PLR packages. Usually, this entails purchasing a pack of PLR articles, re-writing them so that they are sufficiently unique, and then uploading them to a website that contents content focused on a particular niche. Another use of these articles is to submit them to article directories after they have been revised significantly.

Category #3: Sell Re-Bundled PLR Packages

The final broad category of PLR product use is resale. As we discussed previously, this is an excellent option for new Internet marketers who do not have product-development experience. It allows them to simply purchase a product, make minor alterations, and then resell it under their own brand name.

Of course, there are a lot of different ways to do this; and the devil is often in the details. For this reason, I will defer further discuss of this strategy to the following section.

20 Powerful Tips on Using PLR

In this section, I'm going to give you an exhaustive break-down of the various methods you can use to make money with PLR products. Each of the 20 tips below are self-contained, but may be best used in conjunction with one another.

Tip #1: Create a Niche Authority Site

If you're a relative newcomer to using PLR, one of the best ways to get started is by trying to create an authority site using PLR content only. This might seem like an usual place to start, but in fact, it is one of the best ways in which you can challenge yourself to take your project seriously.

In particular, creating an authority site will challenge you to do several things—all of which will be conducive to improving your skills at using PLR correctly: 1) it will push you to find good sources of high-quality PLR content on a specific topic; 2) it will push you to get the content re-written or re-worked in a way that makes it unique, interesting, and clear; and 3) it will force you to put together an attractive site with high-quality products that actually has an end-user or buyer in mind.

When creating an authority site, there are several steps you should take:

Step #1: Select a Niche

There are several different ways in which you can do this. One way is to start by looking for content. If you can find mountains of high-quality content on a particular topic, you may want to consider using that topic to create your authority site.

The other way to approach this is by first selecting a niche—and then finding the content. A good way to select a niche for your authority site is to start by writing down topics that interest you. Many Internet marketers advise that you don't do this, but instead follow the money. I personally suggest that you start with topics that interest you; and then find out how to make money with them using tools like wordtracker.com, which will help you to identify good keywords for your niche site.

In general, you can make money in most niches; however, you will need to spend some time identifying the relevant hot topics and keywords.

Step #2: Get Hosting and a Domain Name

The next important step is to get a domain name and hosting. I suggest that you start by looking at the following site: http://www.comparewebhosts.com/, which will allow you to compare various hosting services.

In reality, the most important thing you will want to take into consideration is the price. At least initially, you won't need a high-end hosting package, since you are unlikely to do anything that is bandwidth-intensive on the site, so pick a hosting service that is cheap, but has a reasonable up-time guarantee.

Another thing you will want to look for in a site is whether it has a control panel that offers a lot of free plugins. Most hosts will offer this; and it will make your life considerably easier, since it will allow you to install Wordpress or another site editor with the click of a button.

Another important thing to keep in mind is that you may want to purchase the domain name registration and hosting services from the same company, since it will be easier to do; and also because you will probably be offered a deal for doing so.

Once you complete your domain name registration and hosting service purchase, the next step will be to select an editor for your site; and then begin putting up content.

Step #3: Select a Site Editor

Now that you have a domain name and hosting, you will need to begin building your website. The easiest way to do this is by using a free site editor. I personally suggest that you consider using Wordpress, since it has a user-friendly interface and SEO plugins; and offers thousands of attractive blog and website templates.

If you don't want to use Wordpress, you could use XSitePro, Dreamweaver, Evrsoft, or one of many other paid or free "What-You-See-Is-What-You-Get"

(WYSIWYG) site editors. The main point here is that you should find software or a plugin that allows you to create an attractive, credible website to which you can easily upload content.

Step #4: Find PLR Content

With the authority site approach, this step can often be hard. The reason for this is that you've selected a topic to concentrate on, rather than allowing the available PLR content dictate what site you build.

As I mentioned previously, http://plrwholesaler.com and http://unselfishmarketer.com are two excellent sources for site content; and you should definitely join both for starters. In the particular case of your authority site project, however, you may need to drill deeper and more accurately to find the right content.

The next place you should go on your search for PLR content is any forum where Internet marketers frequent. Not surprisingly, you will also find a lot of PLR content for sale in these places; and generally, the amount of copies sold will be limited to 20 or 25. Use the forum's search function to find packages that match your site's niche.

The following is a list of good places to find niche PLR packages:

1. www.warriorforum.com

2. www.sitepoint.com

3. http://forums.digitalpoint.com/

Between these, you should be able to find some good starter article packs for your site. You may also want to look at firesale offers on packages of thousands of PLR articles for $10-$25. You're likely to find several dozen articles within these packages that relate to your niche; and can provide good content for your site.

Another good thing to look for is any package that includes reports and ebooks on your topic. As long as the license allows you to modify the content, you can break the book or report into hundreds of articles, which you can add to your site. This should work well, as few other people have probably done this, which means that the content is likely to appear to be unique to search engines.

Step #5: Modify Your Content

It's now time to modify your content. You can either do this yourself or hire a freelancer to do it for you. If you choose to do it yourself, you will want to use a site like http://www.articlechecker.com/ to check whether your content appears to be unique to search engines. If it does not, you should modify it until it does.

If you want to save yourself a lot of time and trouble, you should consider finding a talented freelancer to do the modifications for you. You can start by going to www.elance.com to find some writers. Create an account; and then post a project. If you don't get any proposals that line up with what you want, you can always decline them and repost your project.

Step #6: Upload Your Content

Finally, as you accumulate modified, unique content, you should begin uploading it using your WYSIWYG, too. Over time, search engines will index this content; and improve your site's rankings.

Tip #2: Create an Autoresponder Course

Another great way to use PLR content is to create an autoresponder series with it. You can do this by purchasing a pack of PLR content related to your niche; and by then modifying it, so that it can be sent out as an email. You can do this by adding greeting and closing sections, as well as by editing the body to make it flow like an email.

Once you have done this with your content, the next step is get an autoresponder account if you do not already have one. You can do this at aweber.com or getresponse.com. Once you do this, you will be able to add your content to the autoresponder; and then tune the relevant settings.

One thing you will want to pay attention to is the amount of days between each email. If you set this to be too long, you will lose the attention of your subscribers. But if you set it to be too short, you will bombard your subscribers with emails, leaving them with no choice other than to unsubscribe or stop paying attention.

Another thing you will want to pay attention to is the mechanism through which you will make money. Usually, with email lists, you will do this by making pitches to your list subscribers periodically. You can do this through separate emails (not part of your original sequence) that review products and then suggest that list members buy them. Alternatively, you can announce products as an affiliate; or sell PLR reports and ebooks that you purchase.

Tip #3: Give Away Free Software

One term that marketers throw around frequently is "perceived value." This is an important term in marketing because it recognizes it is not only import for a product to have value, but it is also important for the marketer to convey that value to site visitors.

When it comes to products, the hierarchy of perceived value is usually as follows, where the 1 is the highest:

1. Software & Physical Products
2. Video Content
3. Audio Content
4. Ebooks
5. Reports
6. Articles

What does this mean for you? It means that if you give away free software, you will probably generate more interest than if you give away free ebooks, reports, or article content.

This is important for a number of reasons, but mainly because greater interest translates into more site visitors, more conversions, more subscribers, and more repeat visits.

For this reason, it's a good idea to build up a stock of relevant PLR software programs. Some of the sources I've already mentioned offer PLR software for free, which is a good place to start. From there, you should spend some time looking for PLR software related to your niche.

Again, if you can offer free software to your site visitors, they will perceive that it has a lot of value; and will be willing to sign up for newsletters, participate in contests, and revisit your site in exchange for it.

Tip #4: Give Away Free Ebooks

As I mentioned in the previous section, ebooks are fourth in line in the hierarchy of perceived value; however, for people who don't have much use for video, audio, or software content, they are often considered to have the highest perceived value.

One excellent way to make money with PLR content is to rebrand an existing PLR ebook; or re-work an ebook to make back-end sales for your site. Alternatively, you could use the free ebook to promote your website or promote your newsletter. In this section, I will cover each of these methods in detail.

Method #1: Re-Brand an Existing Ebook

In some cases, PLR ebooks will come with rebranding software. This software will allow you to generate a new ebook that inserts all of your own affiliate links. All you will have to do is create affiliate accounts at places like clickbank.com, cj.com, and other sites (if you don't already have accounts); and then add your affiliate IDs as instructed by the software. When the process is completed, you will have a PDF that will be "re-branded" to include all of your own affiliate links.

Once you have successfully generated a re-branded book, you can begin using it to make money. Since all of the sales will come from affiliate products, you won't actually have to sell the ebook for money. In fact, you may be better off if you don't. One of the best ways in which you can make money with this method is to widely circulate your re-branded ebook by giving it away to list members, linking to a page where visitors can download it on your site, and including it in your forum signature.

Method #2: Re-Working an Ebook

Often, PLR ebooks will not come with any back-end sales mechanism. That is, they will simply contain book content with no attempt to pitch other products. In this case, you will want to retain the content from the ebook, but modify it to incorporate affiliate links, links to your website, and links to your other products.

As a rule of thumb, it is always a good idea to weave the pitches into the text of the book, rather than including them in a header, a footer, or in the margins. For instance, if your ebook suggests that readers purchase a certain type of software, then include your own affiliate link to that software product, rather than just mentioning it by name.

Method #3: Use Ebook Content to Promote Your Site or Newsletter

Another great way to use PLR ebooks is to give them away in order to promote your site or newsletter. Generally, marketers do this by offering to give the ebook away to list subscribers for free. Alternatively, they might give it away for free on forums and list it in ebook directories. If the second option is used, they will normally promote their website or list throughout the ebook in order to get readers interested.

Tip #5: Give Away Free Reports

One of the best ways in which you can use PLR reports is to give them away to site visitors in exchange for joining your list; or for competing in some contest that requires them to return to your site multiple times.

In addition to what I said in the section on ebooks, there are a few additional things you should take into consideration when it comes to using both PLR ebooks and reports.

The first thing you will want to take into consideration is the extent to which the PLR ebooks and reports you are using have been sold. If they have been sold to dozens of resellers and you have the rights to modify them, then you should consider doing so.

In particular, you should consider hiring a freelancer at elance.com or guru.com to create new graphics for the ebook or report, including cover art, and buy-it-now icons. This will differentiate your product from all others, so that yours does not appear to be a simple rehash of something that is available in dozens of other places.

Another good idea is to consider modifying the product you have purchased. You could do this by again going to guru.com or elance.com to hire a freelance editor to clean-up the book, add content, and improve the quality of the existing content.

Finally, with ebooks and reports in general, it is often a good idea to bundle many together; and to give them all away in exchange for joining a list or referring a friend. If your niche is relatively popular, it should be inexpensive and easy to locate and purchase the reports and ebooks.

Tip #6: Use PLR Articles to Optimize Your Site for Search Engine Traffic

One of the most common uses of PLR articles is to optimize existing sites, so that they receive more traffic; however, many marketers who attempt to do this do it incorrectly, get poor results, and then blame the strategy, rather than themselves.

If you have an interest in doing this and want to get it right the first time, I suggest you do the following:

Step #1: Find Ebook, Report, and Article PLR Content Related to Your Niche

As usual, the first step is to find good content for your site. If you have already signed up for a number of PLR content sites (including those referenced earlier), there's a good chance that you already have access to a wealth of PLR content in your niche. Start by digging through your various membership sites to locate related content.

Once you have drudged up content relevant to your site's niche, you can begin the next step: optimizing that content for search engines.

Step #2: Optimize Your PLR Articles for Search Engine Traffic

Once you have selected the content you will put on your site, you must next optimize it, so that the following two things will happen: 1) search engines identify your content as unique; and 2) search engines rank your site highly for high-traffic keywords.

In order to satisfy the first condition, you will need to modify the articles you selected significantly. You can do this by re-writing sentences and paragraphs, so that they show up as unique on sites like http://www.articlechecker.com and http://www.copyscape.com

If you don't want to edit the articles yourself, you can hire someone from elance.com or guru.com to make the modifications for you. This will save you a great deal of time; and it is generally significantly cheaper than having original articles written.

Once you have modified the articles, you will want to optimize them correctly for search engine traffic. Often, PLR articles you purchase will already be optimized for a particular keyword. In this case, you will want to re-work the optimization along the lines of the most current suggestions for SEO experts.

When optimizing articles for search engine traffic, the most important thing to look for initially is whether the keyword is used too frequently, as is common in PLR bundles. If the keyword is used more than once in the title, more than once in the opening paragraph, more than once in the closing paragraph, and more than twice in the body, then you should attempt to eliminate the extra keyword uses.

Another thing you should do is intersperse related keywords throughout the text of each article. If you're unsure what keywords to use, you can use a free keyword tool, such as https://adwords.google.com/select/KeywordToolExternal to collect keywords related to your main keyword. You can then add 2 of the more heavily trafficked keywords to the body of your article in a way that flows naturally.

Tip #7: Submit Your PLR Articles to Directories

One other strategy you can use to get traffic from PLR articles is to submit them to article directories. You can find a full list of directories—given in order of their Alexa rank—at the following URL: http://www.seoresearcher.com/articles-directories-list-alexa-rating-ordered.htm

Of course, if you do this, you will want to first re-write the articles, so that they are sufficiently unique. Additionally, since you will be submitting them under your own name, you should take the time to make sure they provide valuable, factually correct information and are grammatically correct.

Additionally, before you submit your articles to directories, you should optimize each for a keyword that relates to your niche, but is not one you've optimized your site for. Since the article directory you use is likely to have much higher page rank and more inbound links than your own site, it also has a better chance of showing up on the first or second page of Google for keywords that receive a lot of searches.

If you're unsure which keywords you should use, use the previously suggested Google Keywords tool to find a broader set of keywords for your site. If you want richer detail about the keywords, then sign up for a service like wordtracker.com. Either way, use your service of choice to compile a list of keywords that are out-of-reach for your site, but are within reach for authority sites like article directories.

Finally, once you've optimized your articles for search engine traffic, the only remaining step is to create an attractive, high-quality resource box to go under each of your articles. This is your chance to promote yourself and your business. I personally suggest that you keep your message brief, to-the-point, and clear. Also, make sure you link readers to a page on your site where they can download free resources or join a newsletter.

Tip #8: Rebundle Your Articles

One important part of making money with PLR content is "rebundling." This is the process of taking the raw content you get from a PLR site and using it to create a new product that your customers will find more attractive.

In many cases, rebundling is a simple process. It involves taking multiple products, packaging them together, and then selling them as part of a single offer. This allows sellers to offer buyers a great deal without going to great lengths to make changes to products.

An alternative rebundling method involves making significant changes to the raw content, so that you can sell it in a different form altogether. For instance, you might take 30 articles on dog training; and rebundle them into an ebook called "30 Dog Training Tips that All Owners Must Know."

This is an excellent strategy if you're having trouble finding PLR ebook and report content on your particular niche. Instead of paying a ghostwriter to create an ebook for you, you can simply rebundle PLR articles you have the rights to into a high-quality ebook. Once you do that, all you will need to do is purchase cover art, sales page banners, and buy-it-now buttons. You should be able to do this relatively inexpensively over a site like elance.com or guru.com.

Tip #9: Use Caution When Hiring Freelances to Modify Your Ebooks and Reports

Since we've talked about modifying both ebooks and reports to some extent in other sections, I'm going to focus only on one very important part of the process in this section: hiring the right freelancers to get the project done.

Unfortunately for many Internet marketers, they don't pay very much attention to the hiring process; and, as a result, end up working with a contractor who doesn't deliver on time, doesn't respond to emails, or doesn't provide the best quality available for the price given. But fortunately for you, there are ways to get around these problems; and I will discuss them below in a three-step process:

Step #1: Clearly Define Your Project

One of the major problems Internet marketers face when contracting out a project is simple miscommunication. The Internet marketer has a clear picture in her mind of how she would like the finished product to look, but the freelancer has an incomplete picture and needs to fill in the blanks. As a result, she delivers a product that isn't exactly what the marketer wanted; and everyone loses a result.

A good way to avoid this problem is to start by defining your project before you even begin looking for freelancers. You can do this by spending five minutes to write down a brief description of the work you would like done; and then a list of important details that should be included. You should also explicitly consider what should be left up to the freelancer's discretion.

Here's an example:

==

Description: I need a freelance graphic designer to create cover art for my ebook,

"25 Ways to Improve Your Golf Swing," as well as buy-it-now buttons, and a banner for the sales page.

Details:

1. The person I select should have previous experience; and this should be demonstrated by a portfolio and by ratings and comments from past buyers.

2. The freelancer must be able to complete the project within 3 days.

3. I want the person who I select for the project to use my business's existing logo, but to improve its visual appearance.

4. I want the person I select for the project to provide me with at least two alternative designs for the logo before using it to create the cover art, buy-it-now button, etc.

5. The person who does the job must use images that she/he legally owns; or must purchase stock photos for the job.

==

It only took me 3 minutes to come up with this mock example. But if I were truly planning to get this work done, it might have saved me several hours and as much as $100.

Step #2: Find the Right Freelancer

It's a tough world out there for freelancers. There are literally millions of providers from all parts of the global who are willing to take on virtually any project. For those who don't have established portfolios and a long history of reviews, it can often be hard to break into the market. And for this reason, you will have an unbelievable amount of choices when it comes to purchasing the services of a freelance writer, editor, or graphic designer.

This is important to keep in mind when posting a project for freelance work because it means that you usually shouldn't settle for poor quality or high prices. Instead, you should spend a little more time searching until you find an excellent match for your business.

I personally suggest that you start by creating an account on elance.com. Many long-lasting freelance relationships begin on Elance; and for good reason: it allows buyers to obtain a great deal of information about freelancers up-front.

When it comes to finding good freelancers, there are several important things you should keep in mind. The first is that you should permit a reasonable range of bids on your project. You're better off allowing competition between providers drive down the price, rather than declaring that the bid must be extremely low— and, in the process, driving away everyone other than low-end providers.

Next, you should clearly define your project and also make an overt attempt to sound reasonable and flexible. Freelancers will often avoid projects if they suspect the poster is going to make unreasonable demands, complain excessively, and possibly withhold payment for no particularly good reason. For this reason, you generally gain nothing by attempting to sound intimidating or forceful in posts.

Once you have posted your project, spend some time to browse providers' portfolios. If they look good; and if they have successfully completed other projects, send them an invitation to bid on your project.

Finally, spend some time screening all of your bidders. Look through their reviews, their portfolios, and the content of their proposals. Narrow down the field by declining bidders that don't look promising; and begin talking to those who might look like a match until you finally narrow it down to just one.

Step #3: Work with the Freelancer

Now that you have a good match, it's time to begin your working relationship with the selected freelancer. If you've followed the steps above, your freelancer should already have a good understanding of the project you want completed; and you should have a good understanding of what he or she is capable of doing.

The next step in your relationship is to clearly define important milestones in the completion of your project. If you opted to use Elance, you will be forced to do this after you select your bidder. You will specifically select a set of deadlines for the freelancer. In the example above, this might be something like the day by which your freelancer should present her first mock-up for the logo; and the day by which she should send all final deliverables.

Throughout the project, it is a good idea to maintain open lines of communication. While you shouldn't harass the freelancer, you should make an attempt to demonstrate that you are available and are willing to answer questions.

Section Conclusion

One of the most important things you can do when you modify PLR content such as an ebook or report is to make sure you select a good freelancer; and that your freelancer is well-informed about how the project should be completed. You can do this by following the steps outlined above.

Tip #10: Create a Membership Site

Another great way to make money from PLR content is to become a direct reseller. In general, you can do this by doing one-off sales of PLR content through sales letters and on forums; or you can create a membership site. In this section, I will discuss the membership site approach in three steps.

Step #1: Create Your Site

Since we've already discussed it, I won't go into detail about getting hosting and registering a domain name; however, there's two very important parts about creating a membership site that you might not have experience with: 1) creating a high-quality sales page; and 2) managing your members.

The first one—creating a high-quality sales page—is something that I recommend that you hire a freelancer to do. Unless you have persuasive writing experience; and are intimately familiar with sales language, there's a good chance that you'll end up with a very bad salesletter that does not convert.

With that said, it is important to specifically look for a freelancer who has created sales letters previously and has them on display in his or her portfolio. This will allow you to independently verify that the freelancer is capable of writing a persuasive salesletter. Additionally, it will be useful if you can find feedback from salesletter projects that he or she has completed.

Another important part of getting the job done correctly is to clearly describe to the freelancer what should be included in the salesletter. For instance, if your membership site will have six important features, it is really important that the freelancer knows what these are, so that she can refer to them in the salescopy. Additionally, if you have already created the membership site, you should give the freelancer access, so she can do a better job of describing its features in the salescopy.

The other tricky part about a membership site—actually managing it—may prove to be considerably trickier than getting a good salesletter. With a membership site, you will have to continuously manage sign-ups, cancellations, product downloads, product uploads, and membership area content and forums (if you offer this feature).

This can prove to be a lot of work if you don't do it correctly. For this reason, I suggest that you purchase membership site software, such as amember.com, which will allow you to centrally manage memberships, payments, uploads, etc. all from one convenient control panel.

Step #2: Add Content

Once you've completed the general theme for your site, your next task will be to assemble an impressive amount of content. You can do this by buying from every firesale that offers resell rights and master resell rights. You can also do this by signing up for a number of membership sites that offer resell and master resell rights.

As a procedural matter, it is a good idea to separate the PLR content you offer across two dimensions: 1) the rights permitted by the license; and 2) the topic of the content. This will make it easy for site visitors to find the content that they need and that they can legally use for their purposes.

Step #3: Promote the Site

Once you have a good salesletter and a strong membership area, your next step should be to promote the site. Good places to do this include Internet marketing forums and web design forums. Additionally, you will want to do this through other methods, such as by using PPC advertising services, such as Google Adwords; and by submitting articles to directories that reference your membership site in the resource box.

Tip #11: Give Away PLR Audio Content

Not surprisingly, PLR audio content is relatively rare. The reason for this is that it is generally more expensive to produce than articles, reports, or ebooks; and it is also expensive to "re-brand" it, so that truly appears to be your own.

Nevertheless, if you are able to get access to PLR audio content, it will make a great addition to your PLR membership site or to a niche authority site (if you created one following the instructions I provided). The reason for this is that audio content has higher perceived value than written content; and, thus, both membership site subscribers and authority site visitors will value it relatively higher.

Tip #12: Give Away PLR Video Content

Like audio content, video content has very high perceived value. For this reason, giving video content to membership site subscribers; and providing streaming video content for authority site visitors is an excellent way to gain additional customers and secure existing ones.

Tip #13: Offer to Create Niche Sites for Membership Site Subscribers

While many sites offer massive amounts of PLR content, few of them are willing to assemble that content into a workable, professional-looking niche site for subscribers. If you want to give yourself a large advantage over your competitors, you should consider doing it.

For starters, you should begin by working through your membership site subscribers (if you created one as described). Make an offer to provide members with a complete site for a given fee. This complete site might include re-written niche articles; a clean, professional-looking template; unique graphics that are not used elsewhere; and some minor SEO work.

Of course, before you offer this package to your subscribers, you will want to begin by getting quotes from freelance providers. Find out exactly how much it will cost you to get all of this work done, so you can determine how much you will need to charge your subscribers in order to make a profit, as well as how quickly you will be able to deliver the sites.

Tip #14: Create Niche Minisites

Another way in which you can use PLR content is to create a number of niche minisites. This is a good strategy with PLR content because most packages you purchase will offer articles on a variety of different topics, rather than just one.

Rather than just pulling the content that you need from the PLR packs, you can create many small sites that use all of the content. In contrast to the authority site, where you will want to invest a significant amount of time and resources on each site, you should invest a minimal amount of effort and money into each minisite.

With that said, I will break with most Internet marketers by suggesting that you do at least the following three things in order to ensure that your minisites will actually generate a return:

1.   Save money on graphics, but still create a professional-looking site. You can do this by using clean-looking Wordpress themes or some other templates to create your sites.

2.   Re-write all content that you add to your site and run it through www.articlechecker.com. This will ensure that search engines do not flag your pages for containing duplicate content.

3.   Purchase 2-3 new articles for each minisite to ensure that you have completely unique content that will not show up elsewhere.

In addition to these things, you should monitor the progress of each minisite individually. Poor-performing minisites should be closed, while sites with good performance should be given additional PLR content and ghostwritten content.

As far as revenue generation goes, I would suggest selling adspace. You can do this through a number of different avenues, but the most profitable is probably by using Google Adsense. In this case, Google will automatically find advertisers based on the content of your site. Each time a visitor clicks on Adsense ads, you will be given a fraction of the revenue that Google gets from advertisers.

If you opt to use this method, the most important thing to consider is where to place your ads. In practice, you can figure this out by placing ad blocks, monitoring the results, and then responding accordingly.

Tip #15: Create Special Offers for Membership Site Subscribers

As I mentioned earlier, adding more value to your existing membership site offers is always a good way to generate more revenue. Fortunately, there are other ways to do this than the one I discussed earlier—namely, offering to create minisites for your members.

The following is a partial list of ways in which you can offer additional value to your members:

1. Periodically, include limited distribution offers to your customers. For instance, allow your site members to purchase an ebook or report that only 5-10 other people will be able to sell.

2. Hold contests and give extra PLR content to the winner(s).

3. Write a special report for them that explains how to use PLR content to make money, so that they can get the most out of the content you provide on your membership site.

In addition to these three methods, there are dozens of other ways that you can provide value for your site members.

Tip #16: Give PLR Content Away to List Owners

One frequently ignored strategy for improving the reach of your PLR campaigns is to allow other webmasters and list owners a modified version of your content. If you adopt this strategy, a good general approach is to re-brand the PLR content, so that it contains references to your site or affiliate links.

Once you have sufficiently rebranded your material, the best way to disseminate it is to create a page on your website that allows visitors to download it for free. You can then include a link in your forum signature that says something like "click here to download free PLR content."

Tip #17: Use Your Forum Signature to Sell Membership Site Subscriptions

Another easy way in which you can sell membership site subscriptions is by posting on forums frequently and using a signature to promote your site. In order to induce a sense of urgency, you can mention the number of membership slots that are remaining in your signature, so that posters know that your offer is limited; and that they can lose out if they do not sign up soon.

Tip #18: Create a One-Time Firesale

As I've mentioned before, one of the best places to get PLR content is from a firesale. This is also one of the best ways to sell PLR content. If you want to use a firesale to sell PLR content, the best place to start is by accumulating a large among of ebooks, reports, software, and templates that come with resell rights.

Next, you will need to create a high-quality salesletter to promote your firesale. As I mentioned earlier, this is usually best done by hiring an experienced freelancer and having him or her draft the salesletter for your firesale. However, if you would prefer to do this yourself, I suggest that you visit http://www.michelfortin.com to work on your copywriting skills.

Additionally, once you complete the first draft of your salesletter, consider submitting it to a copywriting forum to get some criticism. It might be painful to read the feedback initially, but it will be well worth it, as it will significantly improve your chances of creating a high-converting salesletter.

After you have collected the PLR content and have drafted a high-quality salesletter, your last step will be the promotion phase. You can do this in a variety of different ways, but at a minimum, you should promote the firesale to your list, include a link to it in your forum signature, and advertise it using Google Adwords.

Tip #19: Offer a Sale that Focuses on Limited Distribution PLR

When it comes to PLR products, quality is very important. As I've mentioned previously, there is a big difference between PLR content that is sold to only 5 other people and PLR content that is given away to thousands of people with master resell rights included. The former can relatively easily and inexpensively be re-used for a variety of purposes without appearing to be duplicate content. To the contrary, the latter will need significant modification before it will appear to be original content.

This is one of the reasons why sellers who offer limited distribution PLR are able charge a sizable premium. For instance, they might charge $1-$1.50/article, rather than a couple of cents per article.

If you're planning to do a PLR sale, you may want to do so using limited distribution PLR. You can do this by limiting the amount of packages you sell to between15 and 25. You can also create a license file that does not allow your buyers to resell the content—thus limiting it further. You can then charge a premium for those PLR packages, since only a few people will have access to them.

You can then advertise this package through your current membership site, through forums, and through the other methods we have discussed in earlier sections.

Tip #20: Give Others the Incentive to Promote Your PLR Membership Products & Site

The more that others promote your website, the less you will need to promote it yourself. For this reason, it is always a good idea to find ways that you can get other people to promote your membership site, firesales, and limited distribution PLR content sales.

There are many different methods through which you can do this. I suggest two below.

Method #1: Create an Affiliate Program

One of the best ways to get other people to promote you is to get them money for doing so. This is why it is smart to consider creating an affiliate program for your firesales, membership site subscriptions, and other PLR product sales.

If you don't plan to do this more than once, then it may be sufficient to use Paypal and give your affiliates payments manually on a weekly, bi-weekly, or monthly basis. To the contrary, if you are serious about using affiliates to promote your site and products, then you should either use a site like www.clickbank.com or purchase affiliate program software.

If you use an affiliate management site or affiliate management software, it will greatly simplify the process through which you collect payments for your products and membership site. Additionally, it will also simplify the process through which you make payments to affiliates.

Regardless of what approach you take, creating an affiliate program has the potential to skyrocket the amount you make from your PLR membership site and products.

Method #2: Create Viral PLR Products that Promote Your Site

Another great way to promote your site is by hiring a freelancer to create a software program that "rebrands" one of your PLR ebooks. Before you do this, you should also the content of your PLR ebook to include your own affiliate links, as well as several links and references to your site.

After you finish modifying the ebook, hire a programmer to create software that people can use to enter their affiliate IDs; and then generate a new version of the PLR ebook. Since the affiliate links will be their own, other people will have a strong incentive to give away copies of this ebook. But in the process, they will indirectly be promoting your site through the non-affiliate links embedded in the book that point to your site.

Conclusion

By now, you've learned a great deal about using private label content to make money online. You have not only learned about the different types of PLR content licenses, but you have also learned about the many different ways in which you can make money using it.

In addition, I've provided you with 20 powerful tips that you can use to accomplish virtually anything you can imagine with PLR; and make thousands of dollars in the process. So stop reading; and get started on your private label content empire today!

www.ingramcontent.com/pod-product-compliance
Lightning Source LLC
Chambersburg PA
CBHW072030190526
45166CB00015B/1676